'TORN BETWEEN
BY
Maureen Gearing

PROLOGUE

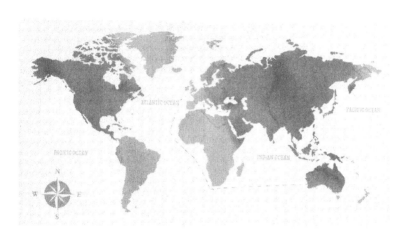

THIS STORY IS ABOUT A YOUNG
MARRIED COUPLE, WHO AFTER LEAVING
THE SHORES OF OLD ENGLAND ON A
SHIP WITH THEIR TWO SMALL CHILDREN
IN 1967, STRUGGLED TO SURVIVE WHEN
FIRST SETTLING IN WESTERN AUSTRALIA
AS MIGRANTS

Chapter One

At the top of the moving staircase at Southampton Docks Terminal Building, I looked down at the family I was leaving behind. I could hardly see them for the tears blurring my eyes, but I could not wipe them away, due to the heavy shoulder bag hanging from one of my arms and my three-month-old son Neil screaming his lungs out in the other.

Having just realised that my husband Tim and I would now be on our own without any family support, I wondered what the hell I was doing. It scared me enough to want to go back, but I could not when he was happily waving goodbye to everyone, with Miranda, our toddler daughter in his arms.

It was September 1967 and we were leaving the shores of England our homeland, bound for Western Australia.

Our journey began on a large cruise ship called the Fairstar, which was the flagship of the Sitmar fleet. It was to take just over three weeks to get there and if I were a better sailor, it would have been a pleasant trip.

Tim did not suffer from seasickness, but it started for me, just a few days into our voyage, out in the Bay of Biscay. The seas were particularly rough and many onboard didn't feel well, including children. The area around their special restaurant was not a good place to be at such times, evidence of which was splattered over the floors and walls of the corridors nearby.

It was difficult to avoid, for the ones who had children to take there, but after my first episode of seasickness, I had to stay well away.

Poor Tim was then left to run around organising our toddler daughter's meals and bottles of milk formula for our baby son, which were distributed at a different location.

After having dealt with all that, Tim then braved the adult's restaurant, to get his meals. There were only a handful of people dining there on such days. Waiters were bumping into each other in their efforts to serve them.

The first stop on our journey to Western Australia was Las Palmas in the Canary Islands. It was unfortunate that we only had a chance to walk around the vicinity of the harbour there, but the ship was not in dock long enough to explore further. It was a very hot day, the sky was clear and the ocean, a turquoise blue, all very different from what we had left behind in Southampton.

The locals were dark-skinned, and most had perfect white teeth, which they exposed in the many smiles our blonde babies received. They stood out when we wheeled them around in their twin push-chair and using broken English, they warned Tim and me, to cover them up, to protect them from sunburn.

The second stop on our journey:- Cape Town, had Table Mountain as a magnificent backdrop. We would have liked to see the views at the top, like many other passengers on our ship, but our children's transporter would have made it extremely difficult. Once again, we just strolled around the harbour area, but it was nice to get our land legs back for a while.

All the local workers on the docks were black-skinned and wore colourful clothing, but unlike Las Palmas, Cape Town appeared to be a segregated city. We saw many signs pointing out the individual facilities for black and white people:- toilets, bars, shops and the like, something we had not been used to back home.

Our first glimpse of the land down under, took just over three weeks, but at first, the ship docked in gage roads, a stretch of water off Rottnest Island a few miles west of Fremantle.

Immigration officials then came aboard to inspect the legitimacy of the passengers, who like us, were mostly ten-pound poms, migrating to the 'promised land.'

Once all the protocols were completed, the ship then sailed on to Fremantle Docks, where crowds of people in summery clothes were waving

Aussie flags, while waiting for their families and friends to disembark. It was late October 1967 and quite hot.

After leaving the port in a bus, we were taken a short distance away, to a Migrant Hostel at Point Walter in East Fremantle, which was originally built as army barracks. We were then allocated a basic corrugated metal hut, which was very hot inside. It contained a wardrobe, a double bed and two single beds, but no cot for our baby, so we adapted, by emptying one of our suitcases, for him to sleep in.

On top of the wardrobe, we noticed a flit gun and on our first night, it soon became clear why it was there, as many mosquitos, chose to dive bomb us in our sleep.

There were communal showers, housed in a long narrow hut with a curved roof not too far away, which included toilets and facilities for washing clothes. Meals were allocated, three times a day in a similar building, which had been turned into a large communal dining room.

In the first few days at the hostel, Tim had to attend meetings with government officials and additionally, employment seminars too.

It appeared, that to get a job in Western Australia, a car was an absolute necessity, but as we had very little money to spare, it was lucky that hire purchase, was relatively easy to get.

Tim trolled a few car yards in Fremantle and finally chose a smart-looking 1959 pea green and cream Holden FC, with shiny chrome mudguards and lights, which cost nine hundred dollars in Australian currency. He needed a ten per cent deposit to secure it, so we had to dip into the small emergency fund, we brought with us.

Having the car made it easier for Tim to land his first job as a labourer, in the suburb of O'Connor, at a stone mason's yard. It had been necessary for him to take any job that was going at first, as earning a wage was his priority, but it was a hard slog and the wages were low at thirty-eight dollars a week. Nevertheless, he persevered, as he was desperate to get his family out of the hostel and into our accommodation as quickly as possible.

We had sourced a two bedroomed recently built flat, in East Fremantle, to move into, but as a month's rent in advance was required and a bond, before we could move in, Tim had to do overtime to get it. Even then, it still wasn't enough, so again, we had to dip into our emergency fund for the rest and to buy some second-hand furniture.

The rent was high:- actually half of Tim's weekly earnings, which was a huge chunk to lose and what was left, only just covered fuel for the car and food for the table. There was nothing left for the things our children regularly needed.

I had been hoping to have a phone installed at the flat to keep in touch with my mother back in England, but that was definitely out of the question, so mum and I communicated, by writing weekly letters to each other.

Our first six months in Australia was certainly dire. When winter came and it rained, Tim had to insert a piece of cardboard into his shoes each day, because we had no money for re-soling and heeling his work shoes at the menders.

The cumbersome twin pushchair we brought with us from England, was not ideal either, as it was heavy for me to push. It was a mile or so, to the clinic in Fremantle, where I had to take the children for check-ups. I envied the other mothers in the district, who all had lightweight and easy to fold up types, they called Strollers.

In 1967 the local buses had hooks along the back on the outside, to hang the strollers on and the drivers were very helpful to young mothers who needed assistance. They got out of their driver's seat and went around the back to help hoist them up onto the hooks. With my twin pram monstrosity, I was afraid to use the buses myself. Juggling a small infant and a fidgety toddler in my arms, while organising such a feat, was too difficult for me to manage.

We were lucky though, that where we lived, wasn't far from a beach. The welcome Fremantle Doctor sea breeze blew in most afternoons in summer. I only had to walk to the far end of our street, then down a zig-zag path, to a sheltered beach on the Swan River, where the water was shallow. It was a great place for me to take our kids to cool off on hot days.

At the weekends, with the kids in the back, Tim and I began exploring further afield in our Holden FC car, while at the same time, we listened to pop music on our car radio.

Some of our particular favourites from back then have become classics like, 'Lazing on a Sunny Afternoon, by the Kinks, 'Summer Rain', by Johnny Rivers and Van Morrison's 'Brown Eyed Girl'. My overall favourite though was 'Massachusetts' by the Bee Gees, which always brought tears to my eyes.

This kind of music was played all the time on the radio and for both Tim and me, some of the music has served to remind us about a certain time or place in our lives.

Even so, sometimes I felt very lonely and was very homesick for my mother and England.

Chapter Two

Our light at the end of the tunnel came about six months later, when Tim's older brother Dan arrived in Western Australia, with his wife Millie, who was pregnant. The health authorities had not allowed Millie entry into Australia at the same time as us, due to a shadow on her lung.

Shortly after that, things started looking up. Job opportunities in the country became available for Tim and Dan.

Our two families, then took a trip up The Great Eastern Highway, to a small country town east of Perth named Wundowie, to suss out what was available. Apart from our men getting jobs, a house came with it too. Millie and I felt blessed and couldn't wait to move there.

Wundowie, a pig iron ore producing town about fifty kilometres inland from Perth, became our saviour. Tim earned good wages at the Ironworks, on the Blast Furnace and the houses, which were owned by Western Australia's State Housing Commission, were a reasonable size and cheap to rent.

Most of them had tiled roofs and the outside cladding was either asbestos or weatherboards. Back then, of course, we had no idea that Asbestos was dangerous, so nobody worried about it. At least our home was painted and had a tiled roof.

Every house also had its garden, with circular clothes drying hoists out the back and the properties were bound by little white picket fences.

The best thing of all though was the low rent of the houses. It was fifty per cent less than Tim and I previously paid at the flat in East Fremantle, which, unlike this place, had no garden.

Our spirits were immediately lifted. Having a real home and an outdoor area for our children to play in, was a dream I had not thought possible for us.

Although I now felt enriched for having these facilities in the town-site, which also included a doctor's surgery and a primary school for our children when the time came, living in the countryside of Western Australia, had been quite difficult for me to adjust to at first. I had only ever known my English hometown of Parkstone in Dorset before, which was a hive of activity.

In letters to my mother, I told her all the good points of course but declined to tell her the bad, like Wundowie's remote location and a bus service to Perth just once a week. I missed my mother terribly, realising then, that I had never really appreciated her before I left.

With Tim working all day, I felt isolated but soon learned that the way to overcome my adverse feelings, was to learn to drive our car. Being able to get out and about, had then given me back my independence.

Even so, life in Wundowie was quite harsh, especially in the summer months. Being inland, it got even hotter than Perth. I rarely had to worry about the weather being too warm in England, but here it was easy to get dehydrated at times.

Luckily, there was a swimming pool in town, which I often took the children to on hot days to keep cool. Even so, our asbestos house was like an oven inside, upon returning.

It didn't help that there was no electric or gas stove to cook meals on in the house at first. The kitchen only came with a wood stove that had to be lit every day of the year with firewood, which we had to purchase by the ton.

The same principle applied to the washing of clothes. On Tim's wages, we could not afford to buy a washing machine straight away, so I had to learn to use the copper with the fire grate underneath, which was housed in the laundry. Like the wood stove, it had to be fed with paper, then kindling wood, to get the water inside the copper, hot enough for nappies and other items. It was quite a feat getting it going and took a long time.

14

Even worse, was the strange-looking contraption housed in the bathroom, called a Chippie-Heater? It too required wood to heat the inner water tank for bath's and looked a bit like a metal rocket with a flexible hose extending out of the side, which then went into the bath. It had no pressure and only allowed the hot water to dribble in. Controlling the temperature of the water was difficult too, but luckily, an installed escape valve allowed steam to spit out onto the roof if the water got too hot. I hated using it. It seemed a dangerous device to me, but the only alternative was to heat water in the copper or sink in the kitchen, for washing ourselves and the kids.

Life in our new country, was primitive, to say the least, but in time, by doing overtime, Tim did manage to buy me an electric stove for cooking on in summer and later a twin tub washing machine. It was no exaggeration, to say what a boon they were.

Even with all its adversities, Wundowie was not a bad place to live, because as a family, we had some good times there, especially with Dan and Millie being there with their family too.

Wundowie had a great social club, with dances on each month, so that us girls could have a night out too, but most of the time it was patronised by the men in town.

Tim and Dan were drawn to the club immediately, as they liked the beer. They had to quickly get used to Aussie drinkers and their strange ways though. Leaving their change on the bar in front of them after buying their beers was alien to Tim and Dan, but they soon adapted, as it was a good idea. They then didn't have to keep delving into their pockets every time it was their shout. The barman always seemed to know whose pile of change to take the money from anyway. Honesty and trust was a big thing with Aussie beer drinkers. If someone left their wallet unattended on the bar, nine times out of ten, it would be safe.

Even so, it was hard for Dan to change his ways and he remained a bit of a Luddite in some ways. In England, he was accustomed to drinking warm beer in a pint glass, whereas Aussie blokes drank their beer icy cold from smaller sized glasses:-Pony, Midi and Schooners. This made more sense, as it was down the hatch before it had a chance to warm up.

*

We lived quite comfortably in Wundowie for five years in all and in that decade, several significant events happened in the world.

*

On the 22nd of November 1963, John F Kennedy, the 35th president of the United States was assassinated by Lee Harvey Oswald.

On the 4th of April 1968, Martin Luther King an American Baptist clergyman and civil rights leader was shot and killed in a Lorraine motel, in Memphis Tennessee, at the age of 39. He was a prominent leader of the African American Civil rights movement and was also a Nobel peace prize winner in 1964, for his non-violent and civil disobedience causes. James Earl Ray, a fugitive from Missouri State Penitentiary was arrested on June 8th 1968 at London Heathrow Airport and was subsequently jailed for 99 years for Luther King's assassination.

On the 20th of July 1969, Apollo 11, was the first spacecraft to land humans on the surface of the moon. American astronauts, Neil Armstrong and Buzz Aldrin landed their lunar module in the sea of tranquillity. The first to step on the moon's surface Neil Armstrong commented that it was "One step for man, but a giant leap for mankind."

Buzz Aldrin then followed and the two of them, spent two and a half hours on the lunar surface, collecting lunar material, while Michael Collins continued to command the spacecraft alone. They returned safely to the main Apollo spacecraft and landed back on earth in the Pacific Ocean on the 24th of July 1969.

Our children were either not born, or too young to have known about some of the earlier events, but for the moon landing, I sat them down in front of the television and told them to pay attention, as this was a very important day.

*

Miranda began her school life at the Wundowie Primary School in 1971, while Neil, who was also very much ready for school had to wait another year.

Although Tim and I had already spent several years in Western Australia, we had not been able to save a cent towards airfares back to the UK, to see my mother. This was upsetting, as I had originally told her we would only be away for two years.

Also around that time, we began to determine our future in Wundowie, as the State Housing Commission, which owned the two bedroomed house we lived in, would not add a further bedroom when we applied. Our children were growing and we knew we would soon need that extra room.

Our best option seemed to be moving closer to Perth. We wanted a home of our own, although Tim knew it wouldn't be easy to achieve on his wages at the ironworks. With this goal in mind, however, we were determined to find a way to get a block of land to start our dream, which is what most young couples in Western Australia did.

The night shift at the Iron Works was never popular with the workers, but with a bit of rearranging of days and afternoon shifts with his co-workers, Tim managed to get on permanent night shifts, which then enabled him to work part of the day at another job. In contrast, with only one child at school, there was still no chance for me to contribute to the purse strings yet. Nevertheless, with a lot of effort and sacrifices for a year or so by him, we reached our objective; the funds to buy a block of land closer to Perth.

Chapter Three

In the hills outer suburbs, the land was still reasonably cheap, so Tim and I chose to buy a block in Chidlow. We paid one thousand five hundred dollars, for half an acre. At the time, the estate agent had shown us two blocks back to back, but having suggested we buy the two, which he said would be a good future investment, we looked at him as though he'd gone completely mad. Through Tim's best efforts, we had only been able to save enough money for one. Even so, the one we purchased had ample room for the new brick and tile house we chose to have built by Artisan Homes.

With the help of Tim's mate who owned earthmoving machinery and a Bob Cat, Tim laid the sand pad and foundations of our new home, ready for the bricklayer, who then spent three months building it. It was a very exciting time for us and our kids, as we had never had a house built before.

Soon after moving in, we then had to enrol our kids at Chidlow Primary School, which was starting its new school year after Christmas 1972.

The parents of new pupils had been invited to attend an introductory seminar and morning tea before the term started, which I went along to. We were asked to bring a plate, which I did. However, it wasn't until after I found a place to sit, that I then noticed other mothers who arrived after me, were disappearing into the kitchen carrying plates laden with food. How embarrassed I felt and had I not been able to quickly put my empty one in my handbag, I would have looked a right fool. Back then though, social events had been very new to me, but I was never going to make that mistake again, was I?

Having a home of our own in Chidlow, was, at last, making me feel more secure about our future in WA. The homesickness for England and my mother hadn't gone completely, but the move gave me the incentive to try harder to make a go of it in our new homeland. I also felt settled enough to ask mum to come over to live with us.

*

At the same time in 1972 though, something was happening back home in England that I knew nothing about. My mother's future was hanging in the balance. She had found a lump in her right breast, which led to a hasty appointment to see her doctor. In his opinion, it needed more investigation by a specialist, who then recommended the lump be removed.

*

Tim had adapted quickly to the Australian way of life, but it took six years for me to call

21

Australia home, although I still did not like the hot summers.

In contrast, the children loved the warm weather and Chidlow was the perfect summer playground for them. With Lake Leschenaultia on our doorstep, it was a sure bet, that when their grandmother visited, she would love our new home and environment as much as all of us, except perhaps for the heat and flies. They were both synonymous with Australia's summer unfortunately and on cue, they put in an appearance at the same time as she arrived, which was Christmas 1972.

We had all been looking forward to seeing her, although when Tim and I left the old country, our children had been too young to remember her. They only knew the lifestyle of their adopted country and that suited them perfectly.

*

When their Nana (as they liked to call her) arrived, Miranda and Neil were just starting their six weeks of summer school holidays.

I knew my mother wouldn't like the heat, so it was important for me to find ways to keep her cool. We had not been able to afford an air conditioner for the new house, but we did have a couple of personal fans and a water cooler, which was a cube-shaped plastic box with a water tray at the bottom. An electric fan at the back blew air over the water and then pushed it out of vents at the front. It worked well on hot dry days, but it wasn't so good when humidity was high. On those days, a damp towel laid over the front of the cooler helped cool the air more efficiently, but the best proposition at such times was always going for a swim at the lake.

Miranda and Neil wasted no time in showing their grandmother the swimming and diving skills they had learnt at swimming classes, and she was very impressed. It did surprise me though, to see my mother in a pair of bathers, which she looked pretty good in.

I supposed the reason I had never seen her in bathers before, or go anywhere near water, was the unpredictable summer's we used to have back in England, yet here she now was, wading out in a lake to join her grandchildren.

After submerging herself up to her ample bosoms, mum relaxed for the first time since the breast cancer scare. She was so thankful that she still had them, which her swimsuit showed off to perfection.

She said she felt alive again and appreciated the ambience of the place. To her, it was just like being at the seaside in the middle of a forest.

Miranda and Neil then gave her a running commentary of how Lake Leschenaultia was formed in the early years of Western Australia's settlement which they had learned at school.

Lake Leschenaultia had been dammed up in the previous century and its natural spring and a winter creek running into it made it very deep in parts. Steam engines running through the eastern hills from Midland to York at that time, utilised it to re-fill their boiler tanks at a man-made siding, built along its northern edge.

Ironically, it had only been after the closure of the steam-powered passenger rail line through the eastern hills; that Chidlow became an attractive place for people to live. Land in the outer suburbs of Perth had become more affordable for people to build homes on, and of course, the bonus for Chidlow had been Lake Leschenaultia. It became a popular swimming hole in the bush, but adding the boating jetty along the deep side, then attracted kids to dive from it. Anglers too were drawn there, as it was well stocked with Trout, Perch and freshwater crustaceans, the locals called Joogies or Yabbies.

After spending the three hottest months of the year in Chidlow, my mother was ready to return home. The ritual of swatting flies and trying to stay cool had become tiresome for her, but she told us, she had enjoyed her stay very much. Another reason for her wanting to return home had been because she'd received a letter from England, telling her that her boss of thirty or so years Mr Trevalier, had recently died. It was inevitable, as he had grown very old, but having worked for him since I was born, it naturally had a profound effect on her.

My mother then had no job to go back to, which posed questions about her future. How would she be able to support herself, after she returned home? I had been thinking ahead and thought it was a good opportunity to ask her if she was now ready to make Western Australia her home. However, when I asked, she had said no, because her father, (my grandad) was still alive and still living at her home.

As it turned out, mum was lucky, that her livelihood was solved soon after her return. Her youngest brother David (my uncle), saved the day, by asking her to be his housekeeper at the nightclub he owned in Bournemouth.

*

Having our young family to continue supporting for several more years yet, it had been impossible for Tim and me to take the kids back to see her. However, a job then became vacant at the local 'El Caballo Blanco Resort' near Wooroloo. A coffee shop assistant was needed, which I applied for and got.

I then worked there for a couple of years and by 1978, we had saved enough money, to take ourselves and our children, by then ten and almost twelve years old, on our first trip back home to England in eleven years.

Chapter Four

It felt great for me, to be back home in Dorset again, where I was born. My mum hadn't changed much and nor had the old red-bricked council house in Parkstone where I grew up. The white climbing rose, was still growing around the front of the bay window outside in the garden and the interior was much as I remembered it too. The old three-piece suite sat in the same position as it always had, in the front room and the long green paisley-patterned carpet runner was still in place in the hall passage and on the timber staircase, except that they were now threadbare.

These were reminders of my mother's financial position. As my grandfather had now passed away, mum's living standard would have dropped dramatically. I wondered how she was coping, with living on less money.

Although my old home hadn't changed, the area where Tim and I grew up had. Over the years, many landmarks and buildings in the Bournemouth and Poole areas had disappeared. They'd been replaced with busy by-passes and main roads which opened up more of the Dorset countryside. We lost our bearings many times, but the new roads got us to where we wanted to go, far quicker than years before.

We took mum and the children out whenever we could in the car we hired and also did a long trip north, with just the children. We headed towards the Lake District on the M1 motorway, hoping to see some snow.

Seeing real snow was something that Miranda and Neil had never experienced before, only on television, so as soon as a largish patch was spotted, we were eager to get amongst it to create a snowman.

The kids also had a snowball fight, but that idea was soon abandoned when their hands became icy cold without any gloves on. How quickly had Tim and I had forgotten about things like that?

The next stop was Gretna Green, on the border of England and Scotland, made famous by 'The Old Blacksmith's Shop'. It was a place where eloping young couples were able to marry without parental permission.

We purchased a small brass gong souvenir there, with a picture of the Old Blacksmith's Shop embossed into it, which we still have today.

Glasgow followed and finally Loch Lomond, which most of the time was covered in a hazy mist. The little white cottages dotted all around its shores, had shop fronts displaying all manner of souvenirs, and colourful tartan items.

The whole area around the loch looked like a picturesque postcard.

It had been a tiring day of driving for Tim, but we got back to Kendal in the Lake District by nightfall.

We then stayed overnight at one of the many beds and breakfast cottages displaying vacancy boards and the next morning, we awoke to a white winter wonderland.

The day after that, Tim drove us back to mum's place in Dorset.

*

My aunt Laurel came round the following day to take us on a picnic to a tourist spot called Hengisbury Head, across the estuary at Christchurch.

I remembered Hengisbury Head as being a great place to visit on a good day, but on this day it was raining and quite heavily too. Not one to be dictated to by a little inclement weather, my Aunt Laurel commented. "If we wait too long for the sun to come out in England, we won't go anywhere."

She was right too, as the skies had been grey most of the time since we arrived in the UK, unlike Perth in WA, where we were spoilt with blue skies for most of the year.

The area surrounding Hengisbury Head hadn't altered in the years that Tim and I had been away, except that it was extremely windy and wet up there when we arrived.

Although my aunt had advanced in years, her personality had not changed at all. She was still a challenging woman, who did not give anyone a chance to complain. Quick as a flash, she had all of us out of the car, huddling around her opened car boot. Plastic mackintoshes and wellington boots appeared for everyone to put on and then in single file, we were marched up the hill to the headland, just as the rain came bucketing down.

Miranda and Neil thought it was great fun to fight the wind and slosh around in their wellies, but for the rest of us, spirits dampened quickly in the blustery conditions.

Laurel had already made it plain, she wasn't about to be defeated by a bit of rain and then led us headlong into a gale.

Raincoats and rubber boots proved little protection from the heavy deluge, with droplets of water finding their way into every exposed part of our protective clothing. We were all getting soaked to the skin.

With flagging spirits, we eventually turned tail to get back to a drier place, but then sounds coming from the back of the group, lifted our spirits.

It was a hum at first not unlike the sound of filling bagpipes, but it was only Tim breaking into his rendition of Paul McCartney's classic 'Mull of Kintyre, which immediately distracted everyone from the miserable conditions.

Laughing at our misfortune had warmed our rain-soaked bodies enough to sing in harmony with each other. As strange as it might seem, the dark clouds in the sky had then parted, allowing a watery sun to peep through.

We had all managed to make light of the return journey and by the time we got back to the café, where my aunt left the car, the rain had eased altogether.

After quickly off-loading the wet gear into the boot again, we jumped back into the warm car, ready for the opening of the picnic hamper.

Its yummy contents and a cuppa were so welcoming, but looking back at Hengisbury Head, it was still shrouded by thick black clouds.

Regardless of the weather, it had been a really fun day out, the kind we think our kids will remember forever.

Overall it had been a great holiday back to our homeland and Dorset, but it was time to return home to Australia, which we had also come to love, so when we left, our hearts were torn in two.

Chapter Five

As time marched onwards into 1979, my mother often wrote about coming out to visit us again. I had been hopeful that this time she might decide to stay, but hints in letters to her were still being met with rejection. Mum probably remembered Western Australia's summer weather and the pesky flies, which she said she could never get used to.

*

Sadly, in the early winter of that same year, Tim mourned the sudden death of his brother Dan, after a heart attack. He was way too young to die at forty-two years of age. His passing had left Millie to raise their three boys:- a ten-year-old, an eight-year-old and the youngest just three, on her own.

*

My mother decided to pay us another visit in September 1979 It was the beginning of spring in Western Australia and the weather was much milder. The landscape was still nice and green after the winter rains and wildflowers were in abundance too. Above all else though, at that time of year, there were no flies to worry her.

Tim had accrued holidays from his job at that time, but this was not so for me. I had taken on a job working in a deli part-time, but luckily, having made friends with a lovely English lady from Bristol, who also worked there, she sometimes helped me out, by changing shifts.

After mum arrived, Tim and I managed to take her out to some interesting places on the tourist trail, including Araluen at Roleystone, and Kings Park in Perth. The weather that September suited her perfectly.

On one particular day when I hadn't been able to get time off work and the children had to attend school, Tim asked mum if she would like to go on a special trip with him.

He did not immediately reveal to her where, or the reason behind it, as it was to be a surprise, but its significance had everything to do with a particular shop in Midland Gate Shopping Centre, we had visited the day before. Mum had pointed out some white lily flowers in a florist shop window there, which she liked, but they were expensive to buy in England.

Eagerly looking forward to her mystery tour, mum had not wasted any time in getting ready. Firstly though, Tim had had to check the car's fuel, oil and tyre pressure, as it was about a two-hour drive north of Perth.

He took the Great Northern Highway out of Midland and then continued up to Bullsbrook, pointing out The Royal Australian Air force base to her on the left as they passed. He had then continued driving north for another ten minutes or so, before branching off to the left at Muchea.

From there, it was no more than three-quarters of an hour to the quaint and picturesque village of Gingin. Tim parked the car on the verge of the road, alongside a large grassed area that had a stream running through its centre. From there, they strolled towards a large old mill wheel in the distance, which was revolving with the current of the water passing through it. After stopping to take some photos on a rickety wooden bridge, they marvelled at the swiftness of the water moving beneath it.

As Tim knew she would be, mum was already charmed by the place. She loved the clear blue sky above and the green landscape beneath and had intentions of painting the scene in watercolours when she returned to England. She hadn't been able to thank Tim enough for taking her there, but as he guided her off the bridge and onto the path alongside the creek, he'd explained that there was more to see yet.

Tim and I had been to Gingin many times before with our kids and this particular spot was very picturesque. Lining the creek banks beside the gravel path, were thick pockets of Paper Bark trees, which produced long papery strips of soft honey coloured bark, popular for craftspeople to collect and then make bark pictures. Layer upon layer shredded themselves from contorted trunks, which mulched the swampy ground all around.

Tim walked mum onwards until the ground became too wet and squelchy underfoot and from there, they had to tread carefully. Bulrushes and sedges were also abundant between gnarled twisted trees in the quagmire, but finally, the floral panorama and climax of the day's outing came into view. Mum had then cottoned on to the reason Tim had taken her there in the first place. She had caught sight of a plant very familiar to her, which covered the large bog lake.

Thousands of Arum Lilies in full flower stood proudly among the lush green foliage. They were just like the ones she had described in the florist shop window the previous day. This wonderful sight had overwhelmed her to such an extent, that Tim then got a huge hug before they headed for home again.

About a week or so later, just days before she was due to go home to England, mum then mentioned something quite significant. I don't know why she left it so late to tell me, but it had slipped out when we had been helping each other with the washing up. She said an old flame from the war years named William Fitzgerald, had made contact with her again.

I was gobsmacked, as I had never heard my mother mention this person's name before. She had formed a friendship with him during World War Two, but it ended when she discovered he was a married man with a young family.

Mum had seemed surprised, that it interested me so much. She hadn't expected her daughter to be abuzz with questions about him, but on the contrary, I wanted to know all there was to know, as I had grown up minus a father figure in my life. My reaction, however, then caused mum to clam up. I did not understand why but presumed that it was because he still had a wife somewhere in the background.

When I was growing up, my mother had never shown any interest in men and none had hung around, so naturally, I was suspicious as to why this man had chosen to find her, after so long.

Those hazy memories of the confession my mother made on my wedding day regarding my father, then crossed my mind. Could this man be him hoping to come back into my mother's life again, or was he another love in her life during the war? In the end, I had to ask the obvious question, but my mother then quite emphatically said *no*, he wasn't my father.

The following year 1980, Tim and I sold the house we built in Chidlow eight years before. We immediately purchased another house at Middle

Swan, a suburb not far from Midland, the eastern gateway to Perth. It was also near Miranda's high school, La Salle.

Our main reason for doing this was to increase Miranda and Neil's chances of finding future job opportunities. Well, this is what we believed at that time.

I had been working full time at a motor hotel near Perth Airport then, but I underestimated the problems that would occur with our kids, shortly because of that job and our move.

*

Since 1979, the last time my mother visited us in Western Australia, there had been no further mention of the mystery man who visited her, during our phone conversations, but then in early 1981, when it was all but forgotten, by me at least, the topic came to the surface again, in a bombshell letter. Mum said she was shortly going to marry the old flame. I had to read it again, as I found it hard to take in, that at fifty-eight, she was going to get married for the first time.

*

It was in April 1981, that my mother and the old flame, William Fitzgerald, tied the knot at the Registry Office in Poole Dorset. I only wished that I could have attended their wedding in person, but it had not been practical for me, as I might have lost my job. Nevertheless, all her closest family members were there to witness it: - her brother Jack and his wife Pearl and sister Laurel and husband Edward.

My three childhood best friends had also attended, as they had all known my mother well when we were all growing up. I was most grateful to them for that and for the letters and photo descriptions they sent. They had each portrayed the occasion in their special way, which touched my heart.

The Mariner restaurant, near Poole Quay, was the chosen venue for the reception lunch afterwards and later in the day, the house was open for friends and neighbours to call in and have a celebratory drink.

A few weeks later, I received wedding photos and a letter from my mother, which I hoped would fill me in about her plans with this new husband of hers. Mum, however, declined to mention it. This was left to Laurel. She had then phoned me and did not sound pleased with what she'd heard.

Laurel was upset because mum was planning to move across to the east coast of England and would be giving up her red-brick council house in Parkstone.

"It's only to please him," Aunt Laurel then reiterated to me, with concern in her voice. She believed mum was being too hasty, but in reply, mum explained to her, that, it had to be that way because William would be like a fish out of water living down in Dorset.

In my mother's next letter to me, she mentioned Laurel's grievances about William, and in a tone that sounded unsympathetic had said, Laurel would just have to get over it.

I had not understood the sudden change in my mother's attitude. It wasn't like her to speak harshly of anyone especially her sister, yet I also wondered why she was so compliant about leaving Dorset behind when she hadn't yet been near his neck of the woods.

Mum wasn't wasting any time at all it seemed. She and William had already had a bonfire up the back garden of her house and got rid of old furniture and artefacts. That concerned me, as she had chosen to burn the few remaining family heirlooms belonging to her mother Adeline (my grandmother) which seemed like an impulsive gesture, she might live to regret. Mum had said, the only alternative was storing it all at Laurel's house, but she didn't have the room.

After reading the letter again, my sympathies were divided, yet it seemed to me, that my aunt had only wanted her sister to think carefully about what she was giving up so easily. The red-brick council house, had been mum's home for so long, which made me wonder, why she would do this? I thought a better option would've been for him to live with my mother at her house. How could mum be sure her marriage would work out? She had buried her head in the sand about that.

In later phone calls with my aunt, it was obvious to me that Laurel missed her sister very much, yet in the letters, I received from my mother, she hadn't said the same.

It seemed to me, that mum was taking sides and her new husband William was winning the argument, although she insisted to me, that he had not taken her away from Laurel; she willingly chose to go.

However, it wasn't just about that. Reading between the lines in further phone conversations with my aunt, Laurel had touched on something that happened between my mother and this William Fitzgerald, way back in 1943.

Mum had chosen to forget that he hurt her back then, but obviously, Laurel remembered it well. She said, his interest in her now, would likely only be because his first wife had died.

It intrigued me to learn this, and of course, I was hoping my aunt was going to reveal a lot more of their past lives, but disappointingly, she hadn't elaborated much more.

I had no right or intention of interfering in my mother's marriage to William, so I kept back what I thought about it all. Mum was still besotted by him and had chosen to disregard what had happened years before during World War Two. If she was prepared to risk leaving her comfort zone to enter his and that of his first wife, then so be it, as far as I was concerned.

As time went on, I learned more and more about my mother's new life, which clearly, she was enjoying. She said she loved her new home, which was very comfortable and now that she had a phone at her disposal, she said communicating with me would be easier than writing.

My mother never complained about her life with William. She was being treated like a lady of leisure and wanted for nothing, she said in numerous phone calls to me. In one way it was good to hear, but in another, he sort of sounded too good to be true.

Mum said she was well provided for too, as he had money in the bank from his adequate government pension and a war pension too. What I did not understand though, was why she had amalgamated her bank account with his. He had held the purse strings in his first marriage, perhaps because his first wife had been an invalid for years and therefore was incapable of handling these things herself.

It seemed to me that he was now treating my mother the same. Was he a controlling man who wanted her to depend on him for everything? I hoped not, because before she married this man, my mother was a very independent woman.

*

My mother and William had only been married about six months when I received a phone call from my aunt, who informed me in Australia that mum was ill in hospital. William had phoned to tell Laurel and then he had phoned me later.

I didn't know what to make of this man. He had a funny cockney twang when he introduced himself to me on the phone and I could tell he was nervous because when he was putting me in the picture about my mother's illness, his voice was shaky.

A sore throat and gland infection had led mum to visit his doctor he'd said. Penicillin was prescribed, but it hadn't helped, as next, she developed a rash. One thing led to another and eventually she collapsed on the bedroom floor, which forced William to call an ambulance to rush her to the local hospital. Her symptoms were initially difficult to diagnose accurately and this was when she took a turn for the worse.

My mother was placed in the intensive care ward, where she was hooked up to wires from a monitoring machine alongside her bed. It was then that the attending doctor explained the situation to her husband. His wife was on the verge of kidney failure.

I shuddered when I heard that and wondered if mum was going to pull through. At that point, I believed that it was time for me to start preparing for a journey to England as soon as possible. The following day, however, I received another call from William, telling me that the crisis was over. The tide had turned, he said, although there was still a long way to go before mum fully recovered.

Later on, I learned more about my mother's baffling condition while she was in the hospital. She had shed a lot of skin, also the hair on her body and she lost hair on her head too. It was an unusual occurrence apparently, something the doctors had not seen before, which made her somewhat of a celebrity patient. She was also photographed for hospital records and medical journals were written up about her condition. Doctors from all over England would soon be reading about my mother and this rare phenomenon.

William assured me when mum was well enough to go home, that he'd take care of her every need until she recovered fully.

Then as soon as she was well enough, she told me on the phone she wanted to bring William to Australia, to visit us.

In the meantime, Tim and I sold the house at Chidlow and moved into another we bought in Middle Swan.

.

Chapter Six

Waiting for mum and William to arrive at Perth airport was a little daunting for me, but Miranda and Neil were excited.

Surprisingly, she looked well, while my stepfather, a tall solidly built man, looked all of his sixty-seven years. He had fair skin and a full head of white hair, which in his younger days would have been blond. He also wore thick tortoiseshell framed glasses and had a pale rectangular shaped face.

I assumed my mother's radiance and vitality, was due to William's good care, so I discounted the judgement I'd already made about him. At this point, it did not count.

However, very shortly after that, it did count. William didn't make much of an effort to get on with me and my family. He was a grumpy old codger at home and everything irked him, including Miranda and Neil. He also clashed with Tim, over allowing Neil to play his drums for thirty minutes each evening. Miranda got on his nerves too. He said, she always had her cassette player too loud, when he was trying to read his book.

The home front took on a sombre atmosphere for most of the time they were there, because William was trying to undermine the rules Tim and I had set for our kids and to make matters worse, mum supported him to the hilt. By the time, they went home a couple of weeks before Christmas 1981, my family breathed a sigh of relief.

Naturally, it was him we were glad to see the back of and not mum, but it had been so different when she visited us before. Back then our kids loved their Nana and she loved them, but this time, she didn't act the same. I decided that this change in her was age-related and that her husband was dominating her as a partner.

Even so, I felt sad that the close relationship my mother and I enjoyed before he came on the scene, deteriorated after that visit. Somehow, both of us had run out of things to say. Our phone calls then resorted to just Christmas and birthdays, or if someone had died.

Chapter Seven

I missed being a part of my mother's life during the next few years and by 1987, I very much wanted to see her again. When we next spoke on the phone, I thought I would drop a few hints about a proposed visit.

Mum's initial negative response, went over my head, but having to next ask point-blank if I could stay at her place, should have sounded warning bells, but it didn't and I went ahead and booked the trip.

Visiting the south eastern corner of England was a new experience for me and on top of that, I had to do it on my own, because Tim had not been interested in going with me.

The county of Essex, where mum had been living for many years, was very different from Dorset where I was born. It had rolling hills and rugged cliffs, yet Essex was fairly flat and its beaches were pebbled not sandy. It felt strange and fairly quickly, I yearned to be back there, surrounded by old friends and other members of my family. The homely feeling of the old red brick council house in Parkstone was still firmly entrenched in my mind, although it seemed to me, that mum had long disassociated it from hers.

William was the same as I had remembered him to be when he visited us in Western Australia, but he did make an effort when I first arrived. In time though, it wore thin and then when we went out anywhere, he seemed to complain about everything. Too much traffic, too many roads being dug up and there was nothing of interest in his neck of the woods. He was a miserable tour guide.

Just like the first time I met him, I found him hard to warm to. On the other hand, he and mum were very close. She believed in him and while that was nice for them, he didn't seem to want to share her with me.

Even though I had enjoyed evening walks with my mother at the beginning of my visit, William and I soon became rivals for mum's affection. They sometimes made me feel alienated and left out, but while my mother was seeing William through rose coloured glasses, I didn't stand a chance. In time, I found myself in a lonely place, even though mum was always there.

What a relief it was when Laurel invited us all down to Dorset for a week.

I noted how excited mum was to be seeing her sister again. They too had been distanced from each other for a long time. It had been five years for them, but now I understood why.

Only twice had William taken mum down to Dorset since their marriage and even then, it had only been to look after Laurel and Edward's house when they went away on holiday. Then just before they got back, William rapidly whisked mum back across the country again.

Getting back home to Dorset and seeing all the family once more, was just like old times to me. I met up with my friend Patrice who I had been keeping in touch with by letter over the years, but it was so much nicer to spend time with her again.

We had both married in the same year, 1964, but unlike Tim and me, she and her husband had remained in the Parkstone area.

As teens and young women, Patrice and I had shared a lot in common and still did, as we both enjoyed artistic hobbies. She had a drivers licence too and was the perfect person to show me some of the lovely gardens around Dorset. By the end of the day, we had covered a lot of territories, some of which had changed dramatically, since my previous visit in 1978.

After the week was up, I felt reluctant, at having to return to my mother's home in Essex. William had been quite tolerable while we were away. Back in his territory, however, he was soon back to his old ways.

Shortly, I would soon be winging my way back to Australia so it didn't bother me, but my mother and her wellbeing did.

Chapter Eight

It felt good to be back home in Western Australia with Tim again, but even though he was around to support me, I felt drained of emotional energy after this last trip to the old country.

Thank goodness Neil was, at last, getting his act together. He seemed more mature and left his irresponsible days behind.

He had got himself a job in the Kalgoorlie mines as a Shot Firer assistant, which was well paid. On top of that, his Aunt Millie, who lived in the area, had said he could stay at her place until he got himself somewhere of his own.

After work, he often called at the local pub for a drink and it was there, that he met and became friendly with one of the barmaids.

He continued working in the Kalgoorlie mines for several months, but then unexpectedly came home for a brief spell. He then left again to work on an island in the northwest of Western Australia, this time as a shot-firer and again earned good wages while up there.

He had been sending money down to me to save for him and I was happy that his life had been running smoothly.

That was until I received a phone call from the girl named Sharon, that he'd met in Kalgoorlie, who said she had to get in touch with him as soon as possible.

It was a shock to Tim and me that she was pregnant, but as they then got back together, we were happy for them.

However, it only lasted until shortly after their son Alan was born in early 1988. For reasons Tim and I did not know, she and Neil had then parted company and he went away to work again. After that, we did not hear from him, for about another year.

When Neil next returned, he had a new partner, named Anita. His interest was now focused on her and buying a house together.

She was good for Neil and seemed to settle him down and surprisingly, there was no animosity by Sharon, as she allowed Neil visiting rights to Alan, as he was growing up. Tim and I were very grateful to her for that and for allowing us access to our grandson sometimes.

Chapter Nine

By 1989, our daughter Miranda was busy making plans to visit England and then Europe and tagging along were her two friends, Garry who she grew up with and Joe, her boyfriend.

She had recently been writing to her grandmother and was hoping that she would put them all up for a short while. My mother had always welcomed my friends when I was young, and I believed she would welcome her granddaughter and her friends too.

Mum had already met Garry from her past two visits to Australia, but I wasn't sure how she and William would react to Miranda and Joe being an item.

At twenty-three, she had grown into a slim pretty young thing, with a mass of long chestnut brown curly hair. She also had a bubbly personality, exuded confidence, and was certainly not timid.

I could foresee a problem with sleeping arrangements cropping up and was not sure how broadminded my mum and William were and whether they could cope with that.

Thank goodness that it turned out not to be a problem. The boys had shared a room and the trio only stayed a few days with them, before they headed off to Europe.

Upon their return four weeks later, it was only a matter of days before they all returned to Australia.

*

Miranda was keen to show me her holiday snaps, which she'd recently had developed at the chemist. The scenery at the places she'd visited in Europe was breathtaking.

The three of them had climbed the Eiffel Tower in Paris, viewed mountain lakes from the highest peaks in Switzerland, watched Bullfighting and Matadors in Barcelona, and threw coins in, and wished at the 'Trevi' Fountain in Rome, plus more.

Tim and I were proud of our twenty-three-year-old daughter for grasping every opportunity that came her way. However, she was a headstrong girl, who'd encountered a couple of failed relationships, which eventually included Joe. Whatever her reasons, she had taken marriage and settling down out of her curriculum.

She believed that Tim and I had married far too young, but as I tried to explain to her, it was the norm to marry young back in the sixties. We did what everyone else did.

Obviously, Miranda had not known her grandmother as well as me, and had no idea how difficult her younger years had been during world war two. Naturally, she had no concept of why my mum had remained unmarried until reaching the age of fifty-eight, so I thought it might be a good time to try to explain.

It was impossible to enlighten my daughter fully about why I did not have a father, yet she still thought I should have probed mum more in the past, about who he was. I then explained, how I'd tried to do so, after my last visit with her and William. Even so, I had not appreciated him wagging his finger in my face or throwing that scrap of paper at me which he said bore my father's name. The fact that it was different from the name mum revealed to me on my wedding day, should have made me question it then and there I suppose, but his attitude was confronting, so, I didn't have the nerve to ask anymore.

*

Tim and I had strongly believed that raising our kids in the hills and not in the suburbs of Perth, had given them a good start in life, but all that changed during their early teens when we sold up and moved to Middle Swan. It was nearer bus and rail transport links and therefore easier for them to commute to job opportunities when they left school, but I am afraid, all that did, was make them more independent. They were able to get out and about, a lot more than in the past.

Tim and I soon realised the mistake we'd made, which took the next two years to try and get them back to the peace and tranquillity of the eastern hills, yet it was already too late to reverse their new freedom. We even had a lovely new house built in Stoneville for all of us to live in, but by then, they could not settle back there.

For one thing, Miranda had applied for and got a good government job in Perth and then had to commute there each day from Stoneville.

She had passed her driving test by then and bought herself a little car to get to work in and so commuted for the next couple of years. However, she got tired of the travelling in the end and decided to flat-share with a friend who lived in Perth.

Flat sharing had also beckoned Neil and by their late teens and early twenties, both had moved closer to Perth permanently.

Chapter Ten

It was also about the same time in 1992, that Tim's grandmother had come to light again. I had been vaguely aware of her as Granny Thom's, even though she had died many years before we left old England's shores in 1967.

Tim and his remaining siblings, five in all, who still lived in England, had become recipients of her will, the complications of which had taken years to settle. It became a valid reason for Tim and me to go back to the old country again, as the inheritance would help alleviate one or two of our financial burdens:- the biggest one being our mortgage.

I had not seen my mother since 1987, so it seemed appropriate to combine our trip between the two. I felt sad, that my relationship with her wasn't as close as it used to be and that made me apprehensive about asking to stay with her and William again.

As luck would have it, Aunt Laurel had come to our rescue and offered to accommodate us at her home in Dorset for the first week or two after we arrived. This worked out well, because Tim's family and his uncle, the executor of the will, all lived nearby.

It had only taken a couple of weeks to finalise the details of Granny Thom's estate and after that, there was plenty of time to visit respective families and friends, before heading further afield.

Next on our agenda, was a visit to mum's place on the east coast of England, which I thought would be a nice surprise. However, hiding behind the hedge at her house that day, while Tim gingerly tapped on the front door, was a wasted effort. For some reason, mum did not seem surprised to see us at all. I then wondered if my aunt had told her.

At that point, William came down the stairs and took control of the situation. He said, that he and mum were getting ready to go to his daughter Penny's place for a week, to help her and her husband, do some painting. Mum did look decidedly embarrassed by then, but at least she said we should stay until the following morning.

Tim had randomly stuck a pin on a map of south eastern England at breakfast the next day, which turned out to be Kent. Aptly named The Garden of England, it sounded nice enough, so that is where we went next.

Although Tim and I were disappointed, that we would not be spending much time with mum, we'd had the sense to see the funny side of our predicament.

It was then quickly forgotten for a few days, while we unwound in Kent's beautiful countryside.

We visited Hever Castle and Sissinghurst Manor Gardens, plus a host of other interesting places in between. The day before we returned to our unwelcome host William's home, we spent the day at the historic city of Canterbury, with a punt ride on one of the city canals. Our return journey was with trepidation, but once again, we did not stay for long.

Chapter Eleven

It had taken me some time to recover from our last visit to the UK, but by 1993, I had focused my mind on more positive things at home.

Tim and I then began the task of getting our house in Stoneville up to scratch, ready to put on the market. We had been living in this home for ten years, but now it was just the two of us:- the kids had finally moved out for good, so I wanted to expand a hobby; that of growing plants in pots, in other words, a nursery.

We looked at several properties still in Stoneville, but the one we liked was not the most suitable. It had a large house on it, which we didn't need and although it was surrounded by five acres of land, there were far too many gum trees.

Nonetheless, the home had plenty of character, with shady veranda's all around and a second storey, with a balcony off the two bedrooms upstairs.

A wing at the far end of the house had been converted into a granny flat by the previous owners and had a kitchen, bathroom, and two bedrooms, plus a living room. An adjoining door led through to the house, but it was self-contained.

The whole package appeared very tenable and I had some other ideas, one of which I felt could later include my mother, who was now seventy-two.

It wasn't my intention to interfere in mum's happy marriage to William Fitzgerald, but he *was* nine years her senior, and I was looking ahead to the future.

In the meantime, I thought of another option. By renting the flat out, it would cover the small mortgage, we had needed to buy the place. However, within six months of acquiring the new property, unforeseen problems with the zoning of the land then cropped up, stopping me in my tracks

It spelt disappointment for me, as my plan to establish a cottage garden nursery on the property, could not go ahead.

Tim had already established his landscaping and gardening business before the move, so I just carried on growing plants for his customers.

Even so, my idea would not go away and a year or so later, when I heard that a weekend market was going to open up in the Midland area, I looked into it with great enthusiasm.

I was a late starter at the age of fifty-one, but in May 1995, I opened a garden centre within the new markets.

It was disappointing that I had not got the kind of support I had hoped for from Tim, nevertheless, I forged ahead with my project against his wishes. He was thinking about my best interests I know, but he believed I was taking an unnecessary gamble at this time of my life. Even so, I was determined to give it a go as it was something I had been dreaming of doing for years.

I had aimed to specialise in cottage perennial plants, as these were the varieties of plants I particularly enjoyed growing and had the most success with.

I then had to choose my position within the markets, which was merely an amount of space, so some sort of building for weather protection had to be erected.

I opted for an attractive wooden pergola, approximately four metres square and had it built to my specifications with a small lockable room at the back.

It then had to be painted, so I chose the popular colours of the time: - heritage green and cream, which suited the colonial-style structure.

The tall peaked roof made of polycarbonate sheets highlighted my plants and allowed them plenty of light.

All my plans were gradually falling into place, except for thinking I had plenty of plants of my own to stock it up with, but it wasn't nearly enough. Before I could start operating, I had to buy a lot more.

In all honesty, I didn't have much business acumen in the beginning; in fact, I didn't have any really, but I muddled through hoping for the best. I was very lucky that the business covered all of its costs fairly quickly and from then on, I was well on the way to making a living for myself.

Although I was happy with the way things were going, Tim was not. He believed that the hours I was putting into the venture, was too much for me and he also didn't like that I had chosen to enter a cut-throat industry. Nevertheless, I managed and was still able to grow plants at home as well.

I would be the first to admit, it was fairly tough for the first twenty-four months. There wasn't much time for anything else, but I did gain a lot of experience and regular customers, some who even remembered me as 'The Daisy Lady,' due to the sixteen varieties and colours of Marguerite Daisies, which I previously grew and then sold at local 'Swap Meets'.

Propagating plants had been taking up most of my spare time, but pretty soon, I'd had to allocate one full day, to buying plant stock from wholesalers, as the demand for different species, increased by the week.

Tim had warned me several times about failing to keep up with what was going on in my workplace, but so far, I had not felt any pressure from the larger garden centre operating nearby, yet I did feel pressure from him, mainly because he wasn't prepared to chip in and help support my new venture. It didn't matter though, as even without his help, my business went from strength to strength.

Although Tim's landscape and gardening business, was equally as successful as mine, I did eventually talk him into working alongside me.

The heavy workload had given him a bad back, so in the end, the decision to give it away wasn't such a difficult one for him to make. Compromising with me, however, was, as he liked to be the boss.

Chapter Twelve

In 1997, Miranda was still single and still enjoying her independent life. However, at this time, she was making plans to move across the country to Sydney. Why she wanted to go so far away from the many friends and good social life she had so much enjoyed, we had no idea, but she went boldly ahead, so we both wished her well.

Spreading her wings, was obviously good for our daughter and after three years of living in Sydney, the way of life there suited her more than Perth.

Next, the millennium year of 2000 arrived with a bang and she was right there watching the fireworks display off the harbour bridge, which heralded in the new century.

Just a few months later in that same year, Sydney hosted the Olympic Games. The insurmountable problems endured early on, such as the smooth running of the metropolitan rail system, and other infrastructures thought at the time to be inadequate to handle the thousands of Olympic commuters, was luckily ironed out by the time of the opening ceremony, allowing the magnificent event to flow without a hitch.

It was a highly emotional experience for most Australians. Some favourite Aussie

Olympians from past era's had carried the lighted torch to the stadium, including Betty Cuthbert. She was Australia's golden girl in 1956, by winning three gold medals in the Melbourne Olympic Games of that year and then another in the Tokyo Olympics in 1964. In those same games, another golden girl emerged, namely Dawn Fraser, who also won gold medals for her country.

In the 2000 Olympic Games a young aboriginal girl named Cathy Freeman was chosen to light the flame at the opening ceremony and then went on to win a gold medal in the 200 metres. Her accomplishment also won her a special place in the hearts of every Australian.

Chapter Thirteen

The year 2000 was also a significant year for Tim and me. He had reached sixty years of age and we had been running our plant business for five years. It seemed like the right time to take a break, so we decided to have a holiday on the island of Bali in Indonesia. It was the perfect place to unwind and it was only a three and a half hour flight from Western Australia.

We had booked to stay at the popular 'Mandira Cottages' in Kuta, a beautiful resort, with lush tropical gardens and fish ponds.

For Tim's birthday evening, we booked a table at Poppies Restaurant in Poppies Lane, but he had also hatched a secret plan with Neil and his partner Anita before we left home. When we arrived at Poppies, they were also there, waiting to meet us at the bar.

We had a great holiday together, and did several tours, one of which included lunch at a restaurant overlooking the Kintamani volcano.

At Ubud, we watched local craftsmen carve intricate designs into pieces of wood and after that, we visited the monkey forest.

Climbing the steep steps to see the views from the top of the cliffs at Ulawato on another day, was tough on the legs, but the rest of the time we all relaxed around our respective hotel's pools or shopped at Denpasar. It was a refreshing and magical holiday.

After returning to Western Australia, Tim and I were then ready to take on another three years at our garden centre at the markets

By 2002 however, Tim and I had had enough, and sold our garden centre business to pursue other interests.

Then a few months later, we learned that my mother's husband William had passed away, which meant changing our future plans.

Next on our agenda, was a hurriedly planned trip to England, to help support her.

THE END

Why not continue reading

Part Four

THE TWILIGHT YEARS

Available as an E-book or Paperback

On

Amazon.com Amazon.com.au Amazon.co.uk

Printed in Great Britain
by Amazon

69233314R00043